THE VIETNAM WIDOWER

Dr. Beulah R.M. Horne

THE VIETNAM WIDOWER

Looking Well on the Outside,
But So Broken on the Inside

PALMETTO

P U B L I S H I N G

Charleston, SC

www.PalmettoPublishing.com

Hardcover ISBN: 9798822960480

Paperback ISBN: 9798822960497

THIS BOOK IS DEDICATED TO...

My friend and husband, Lewis Sr., a Vietnam veteran who gave me much support and inspired me to write this book. And who is still fighting to survive from the Vietnam War daily.

Our daughter and son, Noonie (K. L. Inc.) and Lew-Blubagz Jr., for answering every time I need you. Thank you!

Our grandchildren, Apostle Brandon K. H. Dickens, Bryonna, and Dacoda. Thank you for always responding to my text messages that were sent at all hours of the day— for if you didn't, my face you would see, and the text messages still wouldn't stop. Antwan, always concerned.

Our great-grandchildren, Jayden and Khyrie, and our great-great-grandchild, Maverick. I thank God daily for keeping you all healthy and safe!

Lastly, thank you to my sister solders! Dean, I love you, and Shirley, you're deeply missed.

I wrote this book to encourage veteran families not to give up. My prayer is that you will keep the faith and be strong because all our help comes from the Lord!

CONTENTS

The Vietnam Widower 1

Acknowledgments 27

In Memoriam 29

I was once young. Indeed I am now old,
yet I have not seen the righteous forsaken
nor his seed seeking bread.
—*Psalms 37:25 (Brenton's Septuagint Translation)*

THE VIETNAM WIDOWER

Young, kind, loving, sharing feelings of hope and fresh ideas each and every day. We had fun—looked forward to the next day and the next day's events, no matter what they were.

We loved our country, and we also trusted our country. We knew our police officers. We walked and talked with them. Our public protection was always around, whether we needed them or not; a visit to the firehouse was always welcome. We even knew all the names of our police officers and firefighters.

Sure we had disputes in our schools that even went as far as the streets: some were injured, some lives were lost that could not be replaced. Many, many things happened in our era. Healing time was very hard for mistakes we could never take back—but some of us tried as we grew. But we had fun. Most of us had parents and neighbors who loved and cared about us.

But one thing was universal: we loved our country. We said our pledge and prayers in school, feeling happy and free. We were children.

One day back then, we had a very cloudy day. It was the day our president, John F. Kennedy, was assassinated. And for some reason, notes in my diary of years before that showed a young man full of life, full of dreams, full of hope and ambitions that I had an eye on. He just kept me writing.

The smile he always had, the determination of wanting an education and to achieve the little he often spoke about—which was a lot—and how he loved his parents and whole family. And he had a big family! A very neat and pleasant young man—who did better than better in sports, was respectful, slightly quiet, and sneaky!

No doubt he had my attention as the years went by, as well as the entire capacity of my heart. The loss of his father is only one of many things that hit his heart heavily. He then began talks of providing for his mother and family, even though he was next to the youngest. In school, he was awarded the Leadership Sportsmanship Memorial Award in 1967 by First Lieutenant Vernon G. Johnson Jr. Then he attended college for a while before he decided to enlist in the military to fight for his country—and fight he did!

During this military decision, he suffered another loss—his brother, who was killed in Baltimore City while en route to war. His youngest brother was going to the military, but he did not want him to go to Vietnam—"One of us is enough," he stated.

This was a young man who had now grown older now. He was willing, at times, to forgive his war fate, but could not forget the fate of war because he still faces it each day. From the time his feet landed on United States soil, all things began to change. No welcome mat was laid out at the airport, but the comfort of knowing "I am alive" was a feeling of its own to him—a solace. He had no idea that he left one war "alive" to fight another war to survive and keep his right mind, health, and strength.

The world at home had changed from what he remembered, and time did not stand still. But he carried with him in his duffle bag the many letters sent to him each and every day of his military time, received daily in boxes.

Our communication was strong as our friendship grew, and then God blessed us with love, marriage, travel, and children. I had done research on the Vietnam War, listened to the news, saw some friends who had returned home, and saw many in the hospital. His friends and I paid close attention to his actions, to his eyes. I listened as oh-so-many barbaric behaviors began to appear bit by bit (wild, crude, and unrestrained). The ailments of the war were quickly hitting him—bodily and mentally; his mildness was becoming chronic.

Lost jobs came by the dozens, and the "profit friends"— that is what I called the ones who always wanted to do something for you "for nothing," who always hung around but had nothing. Trust me, there is a price.

But what they did not know was that God had already prepared me, had placed an army of angels around me, had planted in me from birth a fighting spirit, because Satan was not going to steal, kill, or destroy my friend and husband—or my children.

The war at home with all the physical and mental attacks made my friend the walking dead. The substance abuse of choice was alcohol—any type. A drink was a drink to an alcoholic.

Who but God only knows what else was going on. Day by day he died inside and became worse. He was also tired in pain (inside and out). He lost weight, suffered countless sleepless nights, and would often go missing.

Through all of the postwar madness, my angels and I stood firm, took action, became part of hospital and doctor visits, and communicated with jobs, counselors, churches, and his street life. I kept DD214 papers close at hand. All the spraying in Vietnam, all the deaths, all the times having to sleep next to your 'Nam buddies in fields, picking up body parts, guns, bombs, hearing cries for help, seeing the need for help and unable to give it—the list goes on—it doesn't leave.

Many families do not realize that many of our soldiers spend many years fighting war demons long after they have left the battleground. Lots of times, I felt like a widow, like he was dead and buried.

With the help of my God, He made me more determined to keep my friend alive—not just survive. I was determined to let him know the battle was not his alone, determined to keep reminding him and showing him that I was not easily broken. No matter how tough I had to be with anyone or anything, I was determined to be that way—no questions asked. I was fighting a war; I was on a mission. If I lived to complete it, then fine; if not, I would go out with a fight. I had a family to protect—this war affected my children. They saw the stress, the hurt, the pain, the tears... But daily, I dedicated my strength to keeping them happy, normal children. They played a great part in keeping their dad alive. They showed him respect no matter what condition he arrived home in.

Seeking help really was no small feat—finding someone genuine to actually listen was not easy. No one gave the 'Nam veteran or spouse the opportunity to sit down and discuss concerns, incidents, issues, or whatever we noticed in our families.

There were no websites (because obviously the internet wasn't even a fantasy in the '70s). This was the era of "call this number, call that number, here's who to reach," all with no results, no answers. Frustration was building more and more as I tried to seek help. All the while—daily—this Vietnam veteran was getting worse, and no one but me could see the decline.

The whole family was trying to keep our heads above water and not give up on our loved one, but we recognized the whole time that this person must want help to receive help. Then you think that maybe they don't know they need the help, but you don't want to become the enabler. Ah, the enabler. Oh my, we had heard this word over and over, like the war and what happened to my husband was somehow my fault. At some point, the "helpers" pointing at us "enablers" can put their helping power with my enabling to come up with an effective plan and solution to the 'Nam veteran's plight.

The stacks of paperwork and applications to be filled out overwhelmed me—all this in order to be seen by these "helpers." Then came the floods of phone calls, with what seemed like rejections, stating we needed to reschedule appointments because so-and-so (the "helper") was not available on this or that date. Oh, the great pain we went through just to set up appointments with "helpers" in the first place—and so much more was involved. To even get the 'Nam veteran to agree to get the help and go is hard enough. Then once they are willing, the "helper" tells you to reschedule? And the cycle continues—we're back to square one. No rest for the weary: the 'Nam vet and his wife.

But you see, when you know the Lord and have faith, you may tire but you don't give up or give in. If you do not know the Lord or have faith, then you do what you need to do. As they often say today, it is what it is. As for me and my house, you just don't give up without a fight. I know nothing else but my Lord. I know nothing else but to give praise and offer prayers daily. I was born into it. "I thank you, Lord." My first, my last, my everything. I am sure many of you know a song with that verse! But Jesus was here before the verse, or Mr. White.

Whatever tool is available to you to try to save a loved one, use it. Do what is best for you. I can only speak for myself—Jesus was my way. It may seem that time is running out and your situation appears to be getting worse. Efforts for help may seem farther from reach. You may feel battered and worn, but keep pushing forward. Thankfully, in my case, physical abuse wasn't an issue, but I've heard of many stories where that was true, even of our veterans. I pray no one reading this is experiencing that type of situation—if so, get out if you can and seek protection. Similarly, cases of mental abuse are just as devastating—everyone cannot stand mental abuse. Seek help and support.

As for me, I had neither. I was able to remain strong and focus—I was on a mission to save my family and a loved one in need of help. Daily, I was to check in on myself and God allowed me to recognize the lies and deception. Even from those who said they would help. Most of the war veteran "helpers" had no knowledge of what it was like. Besides, they hadn't been on the front lines—they hadn't been in war. They just had a job and referenced books and workshops from "the experts," including the Veterans' Administration physicians, psychologists, psychotherapists, and whoever else they had on staff. If they have not been in war or lived with someone before and after the war, books may help, but only to a point. You must know what it is like to survive and endure after wartime. No book can convey the horrors of what war—especially Vietnam—did to the soldiers, many of whom were physically men but still babies—most straight out of high school. War is death, even if you survive physically. The sacrifice is great, and the burden lies not only on vets but also on their families. Again, no book can teach that.

Remember, this is my opinion and experience with seeking help. It can be financially taxing as well. It is expensive—especially for a young family with little to no access to the correct information. No one informed us back in the day that assistance for a Vietnam veteran was free—we just showed up, and then, before we knew it, a bill was waiting in our mailbox. One of the main things they asked on an application was family size and income. In my case, and presumably in many others, my 'Nam vet didn't even know which day it was. Most veterans just put down anything because they were in need of help and fast. Not all of them were using the VA system. They really just wanted help for themselves and their families.

Veterans and their families in Baltimore City mostly used the VA on Loch Raven or the one downtown, if available. Both were always crowded. Long lines of combat stress fueled by emotions of fear, anger, and anxiety stretched down the hallway of Loch Raven. As the line grew longer, so did the worsening of the veterans' mental states. Honestly, many didn't know what their problems were, but they knew something wasn't quite right.

The words "side effects" were foreign to many veterans, but boy did they suffer from them. Sure they knew about the airborne sprays that were meant for their enemies during the war. They saw it and unfortunately felt it with their own eyes. And sure they could read about the dangerous effects, but Vietnam veterans trusted the government they served. After all, why would the powers that be harm them? Well, thank God for their families who did do some reading and research while they were away fighting for us. Tragically the war damages affected us all—for some just a little, but for many the warnings came too late!

Well we have arrived now, many wars too late. Our children have birth defects we knew nothing about. Families are broken because our government did not take the time to listen to the 'Nam veteran families and friends. Money went out of our household for the war, but nothing came in.

Back in the day, I often had to review prescriptions at appointments, give lists to providers, and bring prescriptions with us so I could be sure the provider was up to date. What a job. At least now, the health care system is a lot better, but

I still do not leave home unprepared. Where was everyone when we needed them? For sure, always be prepared when attending every doctor's appointment. You may not believe it, but our providers and even social workers often did not have the answers to our questions. Most of the time, we were on our own. Out professionals still have room to grow and to learn—especially from those they treat.

Every corner I turned to for help for my friend was often a dead end and a repeat issue. Determined to protect and provide for my family and find help and answers, God provided all of my strength. Love for my friend just did not end my patience—for some reason, it just did not run out. I even asked myself time after time why I was putting time into someone who did not care about himself. Then I would say, "I give up." But then God would allow me to see a brand new day, and my mission would start right where it left off again but with renewed strength. As the old song said, I felt no ways tired. I realized each day that the only way we fail is when we stop trying, and this battle of helping my friend was a task I was not going to stop.

Each day I saw my friend struggling—trying to be who we at home wanted him to be, who the streets wanted him to be, who his peers wanted him to be, but never who he was before the war. I thought at times I was running out of options, but God just kept giving me more and more. God gave me strength to take whatever was pushed in my face.

Often I was disrespected and my ego constantly stomped on, but hey! I stood my ground whatever way it took. Sure I was afraid at times, but my God was always on my side. Of course sometimes, in my safe haven, I would say, "I should have...," "I could have...," but when you are trying to save your family, you must take time to think. I thank God that those "should haves" and "could haves" were up. He wanted me to say instead, "Thank you, God!"

My friend's mental health and physical health were getting worse. The street was making my friend a sponge—soaking up everything. But along with all this war mess, it began turning partly to other vets being jealous of how some were able to stay in their households with all the war issues they had. What makes you better than me? I do not believe your family is putting up with your mess, old man. You are lying about your support at home. Trust me, man, this is not going to last, that is not going to last.

The truth of the matter is that everyone around us, our social peers, was wishing us failure. Once my friend returned home, married with children being born, peers wanted things to be as they used to be—party, party, drink, drink, loan me, loan me. They all had a plan, but none realized that God had already set His plan and the pace at which He wanted us to do it in. God's plans work no matter what. Once I said, "Jesus, I'm available to you," I knew everyone might as well have stood back.

My drive toward my mission was even stronger, and my fight was getting easier. Joy is where you decide to place your heart, and mine was in Jesus, and nothing was going to kill, steal, or destroy my future. Sure Satan was attacking each and every second, minute, and hour of every waking day, but I was ready for the battle. My friend, my husband, was being torn down each day. Once you learn how to be quiet and listen, read the Word, and carry your shield with you everywhere you go, you gain strength with every footstep forward. I had to be prepared for all the crazy things that came at my family's way daily, all the lies and pain. But God had it all covered. I could even invite these dumb people into our home, and they would be so stupid as to come, not realizing their purpose—neither did my friend (he thought he was getting over on me). But sometimes, it is wonderful have your enemies in your space; that way, you can get to know them better!

When you are involved with or married to a war veteran, you never know what they have been through until it comes bubbling to the surface. I can only speak for myself and my friend, my husband. I knew who I was planning to marry, so you do not want to get confused within yourself with how he used to be versus who he came home as after the war. We can never make a person be what we want them to be—that is not love. But if you have taken the time to know the difference, God will give you the mother's wit to know that there is a problem, and He will help you sort it out if it is worth your time. God will help you pick your battles—just take the time to listen. Please don't become a nagger, a repeater of statements day after day. Check yourself first. Please do not judge.

I was a Vietnam widow, but my friend was very much alive and happy in any situation. Yet he did not know why, he had no time to think of why, I didn't host a funeral or wear black and white. But my heart was heavy. The life we planned was overtaken by the Vietnam War and street life. While our children were growing, I did not sugarcoat anything, but at the same time, as a mother, they knew they could never disrespect their father and my friend, my husband, their daddy.

Heaven will give you rain in due season. We have winter, spring, summer, and fall. I was in a fifth-season faith. So do not mess with me when it comes to my God, dad, mom, husband, and children. If you have not found something to die for, then you have nothing to live for. Many people believe in God but do not trust in Him. I believe in God and trust in Him. My trusting in God has brought me though all this craziness of my friend, my husband. Everyone needs to find their strength—that is in trusting Him.

Our men and women come back with PTSD, chronic this, delusions from that, so many complicated problems. To this generation coming up, do more than research—do the foot work. Get off computers and see people face to face. Stop waiting for answers—get out and find solutions. Stop leaving your problems with churches and your pastors—besides, we are all sinners saved by grace. Don't give them God's job.

Review your household; listen to your loved ones. Observe, write notes. If it gets physically dangerous, then get out. Don't stay involved if it gets physical. That is not love. Danger is danger. Same goes for mental abuse. If your mind cannot handle it, then leave. No type of abuse is worth your joy—or your life.

As for me, I was determined that I was going to stand firm and not give up in my fight regardless of the cost. I thank God for my dad and mom. Of course, they did not want to see their only child go through the headaches, heartaches, and the rest. But once they realized that I was displaying all the teaching they instilled into me, they understood. I heard them and learned well.

My parents were praying people, together as a team. They did not have to tell me how they got to where God placed them—but they did. They did not hide secrets. I thank them so much for that because I'm sure it wasn't easy. My parents were in Christian leadership positions, and they did their jobs well until their last breaths. No greater Christian love did they show than for my friend, my husband. To them, he became their son—not son-in-law.

With all the craziness from the Vietnam veteran I was married to, my dad said to me,

"Stay firm—since this is the fight you want, we are with the both of you." This was great—I could spill my guts fully about my problems, even though my parents already knew.

People were saying, "Leave him," "Go home and put him out," "You don't need him." But most of these people were not even married or married to a 'Nam veteran. As for me, I recognized the change in the boy who grew to be a man. How he returned as a man was different from when he left. "This battle was not mine; it was the Lord's."

Once again I was prepared, dressed in the armor of God, ready.

For whatever battle came my way, prayer was my number-one priority. I stayed focused at home and in public. I did not welcome criticism at home or in public. I knew my genuine friends who did not just take sides. I was obedient in reading my scriptures, attending my church home, keeping my faith in God, even if there were no troubled waters—good and bad. God was always there and still is! In our household, we thank God for His mercy and grace. And I, as a friend to my friend, my husband, had it instilled in me to be a good soldier of my Jesus Christ as he prepared me to endure hardships.

My battle with this Vietnam veteran was not over until God said it was over. This Vietnam veteran may have been in the war, but the battle he had to face with God and me was not going to be simple. Sure I was in places I should not have been (in some eyes), sure I did some things I should not have (in some eyes), sure I said some things I should not have said (in some eyes), but hey, as today's generation says, it is what it is. Get over it.

When it came to my friend, and most of all my family—whatever the results of a situation—it was God that solved a lot of it. No one but God. All hours of the night and day, problems would just come at me. Lord knows, I didn't ask for any of it, but God fixed it so that if I was alone or our babies were with me, I was able to handle the situations. But one thing I was taught was to get to the source of the problem. I could not blame or judge others in a situation I was faced with. My friend, my husband, unfortunately allowed many things to happen that should not have occurred. His so-called "friends" listened to his plans and were with him in his outside activities. My friend was a veteran but first and foremost a man. Women listened to his foolishness, and I guess they thought his wife was a punk. But none of them had the keys to wise living. God gives you—if you believe—the mother's wits to see a trap before it is even set. It is hard to explain—you must try God for yourself.

It was so amazing how God allowed me to help others with all they were going through while I was simultaneously dealing with my own problems with my friend, my husband.

But problems with my friend slowly became easy, and I started dealing with it with a smile. I began having brand new ideas, brand new plans—day after day, something was blooming.

To my Vietnam friend, every day was the same, same routine, day after day—same jobs, friends, places. Those things were too much for most veterans to keep up with. Hey, this is called nagging (this is for a man or a woman), excuses, any way out to avoid any and all issues. Blame is oh so very easy to put on someone when you are wrong—even more so when the wrongdoer knows that the person they are dealing with is weak minded because they learn your weakness. Your loved ones, or even friends or employers, know just what buttons to push. Hey, we are human, and we fall for the same button each and every time. Hey, stop it—stop the madness. Stay focused.

Many in war felt pity. Hearts went out to many in war, and many did help others, some let their guards down, some even joked. But remember, many died in war and are still dying from sickness at home through injuries from the war. So much goes on in war, but I can only speak on Vietnam—where my friend, my husband, was. This war affected everyone in our household.

Sure some may go to group meetings to discuss their issues, but how many of us non-Vietnam veterans are allowed to attend? Group meetings are great, but no one knows how the loved ones or families of these veterans feel. For every Vietnam veteran they meet, don't these counselors know these veterans have communities, homes, and families? Everything is personal—how is the family to help? Who is there to assist the family?

People will never understand why I am oh so very happy to have been prayed for at birth and remained grounded in the Lord. I learned a lot at an early age—the most important being how powerful prayer is. God prepared me for many, many things—whether I did it wrong or right. God gave me life and continues to help me through it. I thank you, Lord.

I learned how to lean and depend on Jesus, and He taught me how to remove doubting Johns and fair-weather friends from our lives. So I can continue my mission of helping my friend, my husband. Day after day, I saw my friend suffer with increasing pains, and year after year, they got worse. Doctor appointment after doctor appointment, medication after medication with no relief—it all was the same.

We all must remember when trying to help someone how important their dignity is to them. Please do not take their dignity away—no matter what the age or situation. Why must a veteran have to fight so hard for what is due? They served our country—proudly, whether drafted or enlisted. The whole family of a war veteran suffers. Some go beyond suffering— they lose their lives. Our children grew up repeatedly hearing about enemy soldiers, VC snipers, Charlie, fatal flaws in war, destruction, tunnel rats, etc. They even knew some songs that start, "I don't know, but I've been told…" A veteran can fill in the verses. Our children were only children, and this Vietnam War affected them every day of their lives. The backfire of a car, trusting only familiar faces, rise and shine even before age, Hershey Park, defending themselves at all times, at any place and time, with anything.

It was very late by the time most of us knew anything about VA life insurance eligibility, dependents' educational assistance, and other benefits for veterans. A lot of families missed out on a lot. No one informed us of anything when we went to doctor's appointments with our veterans. And it was not because we didn't ask questions. No one knew anything. The only things given out were medications and appointment times, and even then, we were shifted from doctor to doctor. Even VA social workers did not get involved unless it was by a written order by a VA doctor.

I once was young, and now I am old. The traumatic experiences of the Vietnam War continue to take a great toll of pain. The exposure to Agent Orange, the sleepless nights, the restless days worrying about bomb attacks, being under fire, seeing buddies and even family members killed— it all plagued the minds and spirits of so many veterans. Once a war veteran returns home, traumatic experiences become family experiences. I can only speak for myself, my friend, and our family situation—there is so much emotional numbness and irritability. Criticism never came to my friend—I wasn't in Vietnam; I never saw what he saw. But I knew who he was before the war, and I could see in his eyes the emotionally devastating hidden wounds of the Vietnam War.

I see that same look even now in my friend, as an older veteran with all the illness and diseases trying to attack his mind and body. But God continues to help us in this battle of these bodily aliments. I see them worsen each and every day, but God made us a team and a family. We all work together.

⌒–·–⌒

The Vietnam War was a personal and never-ending battle. Every man who was drafted says this battle stays with the veterans, but this one also affects the whole family with many consequences, consequences that only God gives you strength to face. And knowing that God is in control of it all helps put you though and keeps you moving forward to any and all levels of your fight, through all the health problems—stress, drugs and alcohol abuse, heart disease, mental illness, cancer, diabetes, violence, depression, vision and hearing impairments, suicide, and many, many more!

You fight a war, come home if possible, and fight another for the rest of your life. Upon my friend's arrival home, he often states he didn't see any fanfare or ceremony. No media, cheers, or a playbook of instructions for where to seek help when discharged from the military life to civilian life. There was no welcome home.

As a veteran, the world you left is no more the same, the people you left are no more the same, and some are just no more. But this veteran thanks God for giving him a support system that God put in place while he was in Vietnam fighting for his life. That's because God was in full control from wartime to the return home to the wild, wild west of a new war! Oh yes, he went through a whirlwind of craziness, wild foolishness, and just plain ludicrousness.

But Psalm 37:25 said it all: *"I was once young. Indeed I am now old, yet I have not seen the righteous forsaken nor his seed seeking bread."*

Lied to, cheated, talked down to, mistreated, used, scorned, talked about all day long, almost dead to the ground, nut God was in control and never left His child alone. Wow! A slap to the face.

We all have faults and needs. A care provider is much different than a caregiver! When you have to live with a veteran and see the faults and needs, you give as much care as needed.

You are there from sunup to sundown, and most veterans want to be as independent as possible until the end. In a lot of cases, the caregivers die first—sadly to say—because caregivers so often forget about themselves.

I am so very, very thankful for our children, grandchildren, great-grandchildren, and great-great-grandchildren. They all step right up for whatever is needed and God allows.

We are a family team, and we have faith in God, a faith that didn't start recently. For fifty-three years I have been a caregiver for my Vietnam husband, Mr. Lewis Horne Sr. I listen, observe, be very attentive, focus, and more on the big and little details.

But first, I am a child of God. I may get knocked off my feet a few times, but I will not be knocked out. "Old folks" used to say, "Let me put my religion to the side for just a minute. And I hope these few words find you well and keep moving."

Caregivers pray daily, respect, love, help, find independence as long as possible, and help the loved one make their own decisions, as long as our God allows. All my hope always comes from the Lord.

Learn to love and like yourself, look in the mirror at yourself, learn how to stop judging yourself. Move on from the haters—they are always going to be around. Family, friends, or foes, haters hate—that's their job. And God always identifies them for you. We may choose not to accept what God puts right in front of us right away, but wait for it, wait for it—we finally get it. Thank you, Lord! Trust me, it is all worth the wait.

He maketh me to lie down in green pastures:
he leadeth me beside the still waters.
He restoreth my soul: he leadeth me in the
paths of righteousness for his name's sake.
Yea, though I walk through the
valley of the shadow of death,
I will fear no evil: for thou art with me;
thy rod and thy staff they comfort me.
Thou preparest a table before me in the presence
of mine enemies: thou anointest my head with oil;
my cup runneth over.
Surely goodness and mercy shall follow
me all the days of my life:
and I will dwell in the house of the Lord forever.
—Psalms 23:2–6 (King James Version)

ACKNOWLEDGMENTS

Born and raised in a Christian family, my parents served God's church and community faithfully until the end—Deacon and Deaconess Toney Jr. and Emmie Lee Moore, together side by side. My in-laws were Pop and Mom, Frazier and Laura Dell Horne. Our parents were tough and strong and kept us all in check, and the children in the community; there was no playing games with them. We miss them dearly.

Titles mean nothing without following God's plan for you. Sometimes you lose your way, but with God, it doesn't take long to get back on track and stay focused.

My educational journey was very long—but hey, I made it to RN, then received my doctoral degree in mental health. I had a lot on my plate being a wife and a mother and a caretaker for our aging parents. I begin to get tired, but our daughter said, "No. you will not give up." She enrolled in college with me, and we did this journey together and made it all happen as God planned.

God blessed me with many, many talents and skills, and the same for my husband. And what God has given me, I use. Music and singing: I used my voice many places until illness, and it is not surprising how people forget your helping spirit that God allows you to share. I have work to do and will keep it moving. I was an entrepreneur for many, many years—the legacy God allowed my parents to start. The friendly helpins cares and the cares and the extension of the legacy Kingdom-Living. Thank you, Lord.

Have fun with the accomplishments that God allows because time waits for no one. And be proud of what God has for you. We all are good at doing harm to ourselves.

—————

In my opinion, my greatest accomplishments in life involve being someone to everyone.

1. Friend to my friend, my husband: Mr. Lewis Horne Sr. I often tell him I like him, and he laughs.
2. Wife to Mr. Lewis Horne Sr., the father to our children.
3. Mother to Beavette and Lewis Jr.
4. Grandmother to Brandon, Bryonna, and Dacoda.
5. Great-grandmother to Jayden and Khyrie.
6. Great-great-grandmother to Maverick.
7. Mama to Antwan.
8. Grandma to Sir Charles, our granddog.
9. Grandmother to Bently, our granddog who passed in 2024 (rest in peace).
10. Grandmother to Lewis the turtle.

And God's plan continues on! More to do!

IN MEMORIAM

To our parents: thank you, and we miss you.

Deacon and Deaconess Toney Jr. and Emmie Lee Moore

Pop and Mom, Frazier and Laura Dell Horne

9 798822 960480